This book is not meant to be directive,
I use the word "we" to emphasize I am sharing
how to develop yourself personally.

STOP WASTING YOUR TIME!

Dr. M. E. MILLER

TABLE OF CONTENTS

ACKNOWLEDGEMENTS 5

FAITH AND CONFIDENCE 15

NO COMPARISON 23

THE COST OF SUCCESS 29

DON'T QUIT 36

ALWAYS ASK FOR WISDOM 43

CONCLUSION 50

ABOUT THE AUTHOR 53

GENERATIONS:

"I'm just gonna farm as long as I'm able."

~J.W. Miller

	Liza Christopher		
	Emma Tooks [Christopher]		
	Lizzie Miller		
	John W. Miller		
Viola Roquemore	Anthony J. Miller	Siblings [M]	Siblings [F]
Patricia Miller	Michael E. Miller	Raymond Miller	Eltoney Miller
Francine Miller	Janie Moore [Miller]		
Crystal Miller	Darlene Miller		

ACKNOWLEDGEMENTS

Life can be funny sometimes.

Looking back over the years, I now must sit down and think about those who have had the greatest influence in my life; those whom I need to make sure that I stop and say "thank you" for supporting me in becoming the man who is able to produce this writing.

Life is funny because of all the people I have encountered; my list is very specific; my circle small. But, I'm grateful every day for the gift of these individuals in my life.

But, before I get to them, I must say thank you to God for His purpose being made manifest in me and for destining me to be born into such a great legacy. His design for my life is perfect and I am thankful!

To these strategic people who have and are yet still making me into all I can be…

The 80+ year old mentors I have known since I was just four years old.

To my Mom, Viola Roquemore Miller and my third eldest sister, Janie Miller Moore, I appreciate you for always encouraging me; despite the words of others to the contrary.

To Michael Daniels, the man who encouraged me while I was a young man newly enlisted in the military.

To Joel Page, Eugene Harrison, and Mario Crittenden, who were there for me even when I would text in the middle of the night and require that they wake up and call me because I was inspired and needed to share... right now!

And to my sons, Mordecai, Michael, and Micah, who had the opportunity to spend so much time with my grandfather that they too have received the timeless legacy of wisdom and working toward your dreams.

STOP WASTING YOUR TIME!

Last, but definitely not least, I want to acknowledge the circle of people who have helped to mold my vision and

My Dad, A. J. Miller; Great-grandma Lizzie Miller; Grand Dad, J.W. Miller; Aunt Ella McClendon; Aunt Fannye Salter; Patricia Miller; Dr. Gustave Victor; Mrs Deanne Victor; Mrs. Delores Daniels, Elder Jim Davis; Nathan Turner; Mrs. Juanita Turner; Pastor Jeffrey Williams; Mrs. Cynthia Williams; Mrs. Ruthine Page; Nathaniel Warren; Mrs. Mary Warren; Al Jester; Javan Jester; Kenny Jones; Apostle Mark Jones; and Pastor Victor Matos...

... Thank you!

7 | P a g e

"One day, I realized that whenever I would come to a block in my life, [instead of just sitting down or giving up], I would just go as far as I could see. Once I completed those steps, then I would be able to see further.

This kept me focused and helped me finish."

Dr. M.E. Miller

INTRODUCTION

"Work in the morning and sleep at night."
~J.W. Miller

As my Great-grandmother, Mrs. Lizzie Miller, sat on the living-room couch that Sunday in August 1978, recounting the vast history of our large family with amazing clarity, my cousin Jeanette patiently and lovingly recorded that moment in time; making sure to stop the recording every so often to give her opportunity to take a break and collect her thoughts.

At approximately 93 years of age, she was able to recall several generations of our family tree, providing us with a short narrative on the lineage of our kinship, beginning in the era of slavery with her Great-grandmother Liza Christopher, and included those who celebrated life well into their 100's.

In addition to the roll call of aunts, uncles, husbands, wives, cousins, siblings and the various confirmations of other relationships, she also shared detailed information related to the acquisition of property, homes and land... all purchased during a time when it was not considered normal for a post-slavery black family to not just work property, but to actually own it. And, this they did!

Through this interview she described picking cotton at just five years of age and needing to assist with housework and watching over any babies that came along once her mother married her stepfather. Whether this meant standing at the wash basin in the kitchen atop a box in order to reach the faucet handles or bringing out a sheet to string across the rows to keep the sun off the little children in her care while hoeing in the field, my Great-grandmother knew early on what it was like to make the best use of one's time.

Later in July 2005, my Grandfather J.W. Miller, at the still sharp and alert years of 98, would take his turn at sharing the story of our legacy while riding his tractor across more than 60 acres of farmland which had been in the family for more than a hundred years. With only a second-grade education, he had worked that land and acquired knowledge as he put it, "One sunup at a time!"

Since the time he had been given a small patch of land by his father when he was still a very young boy and following his father's passing in 1923 when he took over the whole of the land, farming was his life. "Work in the morning and sleep at night" was his way of living; his modus operandi.

And, although the original reason for becoming a farmer was simply due to the fact that not only was it something handed down to him, he also labored in the fields because as time went on, it was a good way to make a living and he liked to watch things grow.

When asked how he would feel if his own grandchildren ever became farmers, he passionately asserted that he hoped someone would; otherwise, how would they know where things truly come from or how it feels to work with your hands, milking the cows or feeding the pigs?

My grandfather was indeed a man who didn't run from a hard day's work and considering the length of his days on this earth, that same hard day's work definitely served him well.

I remember not too long before he died, he laid hands on me and imparted his wisdom and health. Along with that memory is the hope that I can become just a portion of the man of character he was. Having fathered 11 children, my grandfather left no less than 500 acres to his five daughters who survived him; ensuring that they would never have to work another day in their lives if they didn't want to.

"A good man leaves an inheritance to his children's children." ~Prov. 13.22

As for me, I was always a dreamer. However, whenever I would attempt to share my dreams with some of those around me, they would speak negatively and tell me that I was crazy. So, as I grew up, I shut down, refusing to express my thoughts, ideas and dreams to anyone besides my mother and one of my sisters. And, even though these two consistently encouraged me to never give up on my dreams, the overwhelming negativity and numerous opposing messages of others kept me closed; creating a lack in an ability to fully believe in myself.

As a youth in St. Petersburg, with my father physically present, yet emotionally distant when it came to me, and my mom working two jobs to keep the household afloat, I spent much of my time involved in illegal activity. Thankfully, after a series of incidents where I should have ended up either in jail or dead, I made the decision to leave and join the military.

It was there that I met a man who began to plant seeds of encouragement into me while watering the seeds of positive words that had been spoken into my life by my mother and sister. Shortly afterward, in December 1978, I got saved… and my life has never been the same.

It is from this moment that I began to fully comprehend that I had been given a great inheritance – wisdom and longevity. Now, the question that I needed to answer was "what am I going to do with this great gift?" Thus, it has been my purpose and mission in life to help people understand how to build a great legacy by not wasting their time.

See, the world at large is in a state of chaos because very few know their history; not only am I blessed to know mine, I have had the opportunity to sit at the knee of my elders and listen to their voices of experience. And, though many of them are gone, I still have record of their stories to remind me of what has been passed down to me and what I am now responsible to deposit into our future generations.

In this book, it is my hope to share some of that wisdom with you, so that you may have a successful future as well. That once you arrive at the last page, you will recognize several critical keys that you can utilize to support your efforts in making the most of your time and to stop wasting it. So, no more excuses; it's time to turn the page…

STOP WASTING YOUR TIME!

FAITH AND CONFIDENCE

"I don't care how much money you have in the world, or how famous you become. If you don't have God or Peace..." ~J.W. Miller

On a daily basis we are bombarded with negative messages, many of which we have become so accustomed to, we don't even recognize them as negative. Our jobs, family, friends, the media, and even our past can all re-enforce a negative mindset. These negative seeds are sown throughout our lifetime and can develop into weeds that steal the nutrients and space our hopes and dreams need to grow; in turn robbing us of our faith and confidence in ourselves and our future.

The good news is that it is never too late to start living a faith filled, self-confident life. Every day on this earth is a gift full of possibility for growth and change. The important first step is simply recognizing these opportunities and embrace the potential that lies within all of us to achieve our life goals and become confident, faith filled individuals.

Faith and self-confidence are a choice. To live a faith filled, self-confident life you have to recognize and put into action key concepts that will challenge your way of thinking, and you have to foster a healthy environment in which this new mindset can thrive. Once you open the door of possibilities and start to actively choose to make the most of the time you've been given, it's amazing what you can achieve!

Conquer Your Fears

Many obstacles stand in the way of self-confidence; perhaps the biggest being fear. The fear of failure will often prevent us from chasing after our dreams. Past experiences and those around us often re-enforce this fear, debilitating us and leading us to believe we are powerless and simply not capable of achieving the things we wish for our lives.

Fear of leaving our comfort zone can prevent us from trying new things that might build our confidence, and a fear of the unknown can keep us from moving forward; unable to build a legacy or a future we can be proud of.

Believe it or not, there is even a fear of succeeding. If we do get that big promotion, will we be able to handle the responsibility? If we do write that novel we've always dreamed of writing, how will people respond to it? A fear of change may keep us safe in our nest of comfort, but we will never know what it is like to fully spread our wings and fly.

Conquering these fears is an important first step to building faith and self-confidence. Many of us may not even realize we allow these fears to control our lives, nor understand the consequences of giving control to such fears.

Becoming comfortable with the possibility of failure, opening yourself up to try new things, and even learning to accept success are all part of the journey toward a more confident, faith-filled life. Once we learn to let go of fear, life becomes an experience rather than just an existence, and every day becomes a gift that is ripe with potential and opportunity.

Break the Habit of Negativity

We all have that friend or family member who views the world with a glass half empty mentality. Surrounding ourselves with negative people and thoughts can not only have a damaging effect on our health and happiness, it can also prevent us from having faith in ourselves and our future.

When we share our hopes and dreams with those who are not supportive, we expose ourselves to a closed-door attitude that says we will never be good enough or capable enough to achieve what we hope for ourselves. Even the most resilient of hearts cannot help but be discouraged by this type of negativity. Removing it from our lives, whether by making it clear to friends or family that you no longer wish to hear negative comments, or in extreme cases, removing that friend or relation from your life altogether, will give you the space to grow in a more positive direction.

Bad things happen to good people and we will all face negative situations throughout the course of our lives. The important thing is how we respond to these situations. A negative attitude does little to grow faith and hope in trying times. Why focus your energy on negative thoughts that only make the situation worse when you could instead look for the silver lining?

It may sound a bit cliché, but it's true – In all things give thanks. By practicing thankfulness in any given situation, you will break the habit of negativity and discover a positive mindset, even in the most difficult circumstances; giving you the resilience to overcome any challenge life may throw your way and the determination to make your dreams a reality.

Move Beyond Your Past

Our past experiences can also have a negative impact on our belief in ourselves and a viable future. Whether you grew up hearing that you weren't capable enough to achieve your goals or simply had a bad experience that shaped the way you view yourself, not allowing your past to dictate your future is an important part of building self-confidence and making the most of the time you are given on this earth.

Seeking Approval

It's natural to seek approval and acceptance from others, but when we seek validation for the wrong reasons, it can hamper our growth and sap our self-confidence. Being true to yourself is the only way to be truly happy and confident with who you are; even if that means going against the crowd.

When you are true to yourself, you are fulfilling your unique life mission. Your beliefs and dreams are just as valid as everyone else's. Remind yourself of this the next time you find yourself seeking approval from others and know that it is ok to sometimes choose your own path; even if it is the one less traveled or no one else is doing it.

Change Your Environment!

A healthy environment is key to building faith and self-confidence. This means removing yourself from negative habits and influences, such as the naysayers we discussed earlier who work to discourage rather than encourage you in fulfilling your dreams.

A pessimistic atmosphere will get you nowhere if you are trying to build faith and self-confidence. Remember, *"Birds of a feather flock together."* So, sometimes you will absolutely need to do something as simple as shift your position and, moving your seat or something as drastic as changing jobs or relocating. This doesn't mean that you don't love or care for the ones you are distancing yourself from, it just means that you value who you are and what you are trying to do enough to make the necessary changes and to do the hard thing that's required.

STOP WASTING YOUR TIME! Your future is just that – yours. Ultimately, you are the only one responsible for your happiness and success. Whether you choose to live your life with faith and self-confidence or despair and self-doubt is up to you. But, one thing is certain – wishing for a better life doesn't make it so.

You have to possess the needed faith and self-confidence to champion an optimistic lifestyle; making the most of every moment you have been given to persistently pursue your best outcome in a world that will often oppose you. You need to create an environment that supports you while you embrace the opportunities available to you each and every day, so that you can go on and achieve great things.

"By humility and the fear of the Lord are riches, and honor, and life."
~Prov. 22:4 KJV

NO COMPARISON
"The grass may be greener on the other side,
but you still got to cut it!"
~M.E. Miller

So, you're working hard at keeping your lawn neat and trimmed, free of weeds and cut weekly. Then one day you happen to glance over the fence at your neighbor's yard, finding it expertly landscaped and worthy of a Better Homes and Gardens magazine cover.

And your esteem is instantly deflated.

Looking over your yard, you begin to feel as if all of your hard work is for nothing, because it will never look as good as theirs. What's the point? You become conscious that you are experiencing characteristics of envy, jealousy or inadequacy.

Of course, most people wouldn't get sidetracked over something as simple as this. But, consider this as just one example and take a moment to reflect on a time when you took note of someone who seemed more accomplished, more attractive, or appeared more financially successful than you... perhaps they were gaining notoriety or awards in an area you desired or receiving greater celebrity than you. Did you feel the same as in our example?

Did you see your contribution as inferior or worthless? Did you either throw your hands up in defeat or experience stress, anxiety or depression? Or, perhaps you began to speak poorly of the other person's achievements; making their efforts look small in the eyes of others?

"A flower doesn't think of competing to the flower next to it. It just blooms." ~Unknown

Although it is human tendency to want nothing but the best, consistently comparing our lives to our neighbors or colleagues will only cause us to operate at a level of discontent (or even pride) that can short-circuit our progress and stop us from attaining our best and highest dreams.

Everyone has his or her share of pluses and minuses. If you keep comparing yourself to others, you will undoubtedly focus on the negatives; creating feelings of insufficiency or an underlying belief that your efforts are insignificant.

"I will praise thee; for I am fearfully and wonderfully made..." ~Psalm 139:14

Research has proven that people who compare themselves to others will go to extreme measures to acquire whatever they feel is lacking. That's why it's critical to have a healthy esteem of ourselves and others.

Take Action
People like my Great-grandmother and grandfather, who made the most of their every waking hour, are willing to do the hard work. Unfortunately, others would prefer to just sit and complain about how hard things are,

rather than push through their difficulties in order to accomplish the level of success they see in others. Don't be as one of those, as it only leads to dissatisfaction; de-motivating you and ensuring that you lose focus on the quality of life and relationships that you already have and should be enjoying.

Get Understanding
Most people make a point of presenting a happy face even though there's turmoil going on in their personal life. Just check with anyone as to "How are they feeling today?" The majority will simply put on a cheerful smile and say "great", "good" or "all is well".

Very few people will stop and tell you how they really feel or share with you all the problems they are facing (unless you are an extremely close friend). Instead, they will make it a point to paint a very rosy picture.

So, when you compare yourself to someone else you are doing so with little or no real information as to the reality of their life.

Be Grateful

You need to remember the good things you already have in your life. The wise have always said: As long as you have a roof above your head, food on the table and clothes on your body, you are taken care of. Anything beyond that is a luxury. As the old gospel song says: "Count your many blessings... name them one by one. And, it will surprise you what the Lord has done."

In other words, be mindful of all that you have as opposed to what you think you should have as compared to what someone else has.

> *"I once cried because I had no shoes,*
> *until I met a man who had no feet."*
> ~Indian Proverb

STOP WASTING YOUR TIME! At the end of the day, there are four conditions we will experience in our life that innately causes suffering: Birth, Aging, Illness and Death. Of all the inhabitants of this earth, there is not one of us who will not have to experience these;

not one can escape this truth! It doesn't matter how rich, or powerful, or beautiful, or successful...

Therefore, always be mindful that just because something glitters, doesn't mean its pure gold! External 'stuff' is superficial and can be stolen, lost, or faded. The greater gift is the value of those intangible qualities and strengths that support us in becoming all that we were created to be. Pursue this with all zeal rather than constantly looking around you to see what everyone else has and is doing.

"Blessed is the man that walks not in the counsel of the ungodly, nor stands in the way of sinners, nor sits in the seat of the scornful. But his delight is in the law of the Lord; and in his law doth he meditate day and night. And he shall be like a tree planted by the rivers of water, that bringeth forth his fruit in his season; his leaf also shall not wither; and whatsoever he doeth shall prosper."
~Psalms 1:1-3

THE COST OF SUCCESS

"If a man is willing to wait,
he can have what he wants."
~J.W. Miller

Everyone has goals for their life that in some form or another involves being successful in its pursuit. Whether we want to complete a college education, excel in a sport, own our own business, or simply lose weight, life goals require that we give something of ourselves to make our dreams a reality.

"The price of success is hard work, dedication to the job at hand, and the determination that whether we win or lose, we have applied the best of ourselves to the task at hand." ~Vince Lombardi

Deciding to commit to the success of something we want is exciting, at least in the beginning... before the challenges set in. But more often than not, we are quick to idealize what we want in life without first considering what is at stake, often leaving us with abandoned goals because of disillusionment while finding ourselves living an unfulfilled life.

Mankind's belief in success is commendable, but often flawed. The perfect example of this is New Year's Eve resolutions. How many of us have set out with the heartfelt intention to keep our resolutions, yet break them a few weeks or even days later? We decide to accomplish great things without really considering first the cost of the success we are pursuing. Not long after we set out to conquer the world, and we find ourselves frustrated and quickly defeated.

Consider the Sacrifice
So, how do we accomplish success effectively? Before setting goals for success, it's important to first consider the sacrifices that will be required. Giving up the things we love isn't easy, but it's an important part of achieving life goals. If we aren't willing to make sacrifices for success, than we can't give the best of ourselves and be truly passionate about what we are striving to achieve.

By taking the time to consider what will be required to reach a goal, we ensure a more committed dedication to attain what we set out to do, ensuring we are less likely to get discouraged with our inability to make things happen and more likely to attain success.

It's a good thing that we have to work hard for what we want in life! How else would we know if something is really worth fighting for? Sacrifice challenges us, pushes us, and draws a clear line between what we think we want in life and what we truly need.

Commitment to something we truly need means the sacrifices are worth it in the end, and we won't stop trying simply because the road gets a bit rough before we cross the finish line.

Failure Is Part of Success

Before we commit to a goal, it's also extremely important to realize failure is an integral part of success. J K Rowling's first Harry Potter manuscript was rejected 12 times before a publisher recognized its potential. Steven Spielberg was rejected by the University of Southern California School of Cinematic Arts more than once. Van Gogh, despite his world renown today, never knew success during his lifetime. In fact, he only sold one painting shortly before his death, yet he continued to paint because he was passionate about his visionary art.

When you set out to accomplish something, it's important to know that success cannot be achieved without a passionate dedication to your goal, even when it seems as if you will never succeed.

To be dedicated, you have to have a true passion for your goal that goes beyond succeeding.

Most innovators face many failures on the road to success; however, no matter how many times failure sets them back, they continue to create because they love what they are doing and recognize their passions for their own integral worth, with or without success.

Earning Success

We've all known people who seemingly have success handed to them on a silver platter and have all felt envious of the privilege or good luck that got them places we wish we could be, but the truth is there is much more reward in earning your success than having it handed to you. When we earn success, we develop and apply the best of who we are, giving us a satisfaction that far outweighs simply being given what we want.

In the midst of the challenges and sacrifices we may face on the road to success, we may wish for an easier path, but in the end, it's the road we take – the one riddled with challenges and sacrifices – that builds character, pushes us to become stronger people, and makes us more grateful for success when it comes.

Maintain Your Balance

Success takes sacrifice but should never come at the cost of your personal life, health, or the well-being of others. There's a fine balance between pushing yourself to succeed and pushing yourself beyond your capabilities. If you find you are no longer passionate about your goal or are increasingly unhappy with the sacrifices you have to make to succeed, perhaps it's time to re-evaluate your game plan.

"I am come that they might have life, and that they might have it more abundantly."
~John 10:10b

Seek to find new ways to succeed at your goals, and if that's not possible, consider what your life would be like if you didn't achieve the goal you set out to obtain; perhaps success in this instance isn't as important as you first believed it to be.

There's nothing wrong with deciding a particular road just isn't part of your life plan anymore. Perhaps your passions have changed, or circumstances have made you take a new path. It's better to know your boundaries and admit success isn't possible sometimes than to sacrifice your well-being and happiness for a lost cause or unachievable goal.

STOP WASTING YOUR TIME!

Forming a solid commitment, working hard, and seeing our goals through to the end gives us a unique sense of achievement that is one of the best feelings in the world. But before we strive to reach for the stars, we have to first ensure we can stand on our own two feet. Have a game plan when you set goals.

Have a clear understanding of the sacrifices involved and measure your passion to ensure the effort is worthy of your commitment. Success requires hard work, dedication, and the ability to accept failure and keep going. Once you discover the things you are passionate about and find a committed path to life goals, nothing can stop you from succeeding!

"For God sent not his Son into the world to condemn the world; but that the world through him might be saved." ~John 3:17

DON'T QUIT
"Live your life to the best of your ability."
~Lizzie Miller

Prior to going into the military, I remember one of my siblings saying to me that due to my issues with anger, I wouldn't make it one day! In essence, she was saying that my success in the Armed Forces would be impossible, but instead of allowing these words to stop me... I used them to fire me up; fueling a resolve that eventually led to my retiring 20 years later with a successful career in the United States Air Force.

I share this testimony for all those who allow obstacles, distractions or mistakes to stop them in their tracks. Had Edison quit after experiencing 10,000 unsuccessful attempts before finally enlisting the assistance of Lewis

Latimer, the light bulb would never have seen the light of day. Had Henry Ford stopped when funding was exhausted, and he couldn't obtain any more loans to complete development of the assembly line technique to produce the Model T, the way we travel today may never have become a reality. Had Dr. Martin Luther King, Jr. quit after facing countless forces of opposition and being placed in jail numerous times, the civil rights movement would have stalled long before certain rights were won for an entire nation of disenfranchised people.

If you have lived on this earth for more than a few years, you will have undoubtedly suffered some form of setback, encountered seemingly insurmountable odds, or fallen. We all have. However, rather than lie down in the dust and die with dreams unrealized, get up, dust yourself off and continue to press towards your goal. You've only failed, when you cease to do so...

"Fall seven times. Stand up eight."
~Unknown

One of the most important factors that will lead to your ability to accomplish the vision you have for your life is to keep pushing despite the opposition you find yourself coming up against. To throw up your hands and say "it's too hard" is simply a justification for your failure; an excuse. Instead, determine to not just start, but to finish... and to finish well.

"Go as far as you can and when you get there, you will see further." ~Unknown

Like building muscle in the gym, pushing through the "hard stuff" increases strength; allowing you to become resilient and capable of great things due to the challenges you have overcome. It is exactly the challenges you face that create the ability needed to respond to new opportunities and growth. Never allow your hardships to control your destiny. Rather, learn and grow from them. Like Friedrich Nietzsche said, *"That which does not kill us makes us stronger."*

A primary way to stop wasting your time because you quit each time you encounter hardships and distractions, is to keep the vision before you at all times. Here are some tried and true actions you can take today:

Write it Down

Write your dream everywhere you can see it. Put it on a piece of paper on your bedside table, on sticky notes on your refrigerator, on index cards you carry with you, or even taped to your bathroom mirror to read every time you wash your face...

"Write the vision and make it plain on tablets, That he may run who reads it." ~Hab. 2:2

Review written plans daily and make sure activities are included that support your goals; even if for just 10 or 30 minutes a day. I call these my Increasers... they are what allow me to have increase in my life on my terms. This will also help to keep you encouraged and give you a source of strength and focus.

Maintain a journal or notebook and write detailed notes and thoughts as they come to you; no matter how miniscule. Whether this is done with traditional pen and paper, via a voice recording device, or in a phone app, it is a great way of capturing ideas and impressions that can be easily retrieved later.

Get an Accountability Partner
Tony Robbins, a well-known life coach and motivational speaker, in his bestselling book "Awaken the Giant Within", stated the following:

"If I'm committed, there is always a way."

Robbins has also been quoted saying, *"You should demand more from yourself, than anyone else could ever expect."* Therefore, there is no one who is going to know, better than you, how committed you are (or are not) to your vision.

You'll know whether you hit the milestones or cheated. You'll know if you showed up to last week's training sessions or not. And, you'll know whether you made the tough decision to get up and do the hard work or chose instead to just sleep in. Only you will know.

However, self-monitoring can only go so far. Including an objective party in your plan, who can act as both a checkpoint and a cheerleader, will be a great support to help prevent you from giving up or giving in. It's in this way that having an accountability partner is extremely helpful to staying your course when things get 'hard' and you want to quit. See, it's too easy to sabotage your own effort if there's no accountability.

What exactly is an accountability partner? An accountability partner is a person who will coach you over a set period of time for the purpose of helping you keep a commitment; someone who will assist you in adhering to your stated goals. This relationship could be as formal as a Life Coach, a Mentor or a Personal Trainer. Or, it could be less formal with a family member, or a supportive friend.

Celebrate Your Accomplishments

Often, we get so caught up in trying to succeed at something that we lose sight of how far we have actually come. Taking a moment to acknowledge the achievement of milestones along the way is great for providing motivation and is an encouragement to keep moving forward and write them down! Put them on a calendar, memorialize them.

STOP WASTING YOUR TIME! There are many reasons as to why you should never give up; yet, the most valuable is because you were created with purpose and this purpose must be expressed and manifested. Yet, what stops most people, unfortunately is the belief that the vision that was breathed into them will be impossible to birth.

Rather than accepting that thought, think of it this way: The very word impossible says, **"I'M POSSIBLE!"** Realize that at the end of the day, you alone are responsible for your own success or failure. The idea that someone owes you an easy road or that you're entitled to being

STOP WASTING YOUR TIME!

handed a great life, is a false one. So, Buckle up, dig in and do the work.

"God is our refuge and strength,
a very present help in trouble." ~Psalm 46:1

ALWAYS ASK FOR WISDOM
"You're never totally grown; as long as you live, you'll need somebody to guide you. So, don't ever think you won't need someone... even if it's nothing more than a drink of water." ~J. W. Miller

The world is such a strange place. Most of the people out there are part of a crab-like culture. If you see a few crabs in a basket, you will find a few crabs trying to come out of the basket. Unfortunately, the others in the basket will grab the crabs and pull them back in. In the same way, those around you who do not have the motivation to create something amazing in their life, will instead create hurdles to make sure you don't achieve your highest dreams.

43 | P a g e

This is why it is critical to surround yourself with the support of family, friends and colleagues who either have traveled the road you're on, accomplished what you're working toward, or truly believe that you can do whatever you set your mind and heart to do. Without question, having a system of support, composed of professional and personal relationships you can look to for wise counsel, a sounding board or even a heart-check in love, can be incredibly beneficial and advantageous to one's success.

"People seldom improve when they have no other model but themselves to copy."
~Oliver Goldsmith

Always be mindful that you cannot learn everything you need to grow and succeed while living in isolation. You should always be open to the wisdom of a trusted set of advisors. I would not know what I know today, if not for the wisdom of my close friends and Elders… some at whose feet I still sit today! Before I sign a contract or if I'm working through a difficult program or project, I have no problem reaching out for wisdom.

If you believe you know everything and no longer require any knowledge from anyone else, then you are putting yourself at a huge disadvantage. By continually refusing counsel or lacking a willingness to seek it out, you just may discover that there isn't anyone desiring to share with you when you need it the most. So, it is essential that you work on overcoming any stubbornness in your attitude regarding receiving guidance from others.

However, the relationship isn't meant to only operate one way. Your support system isn't just about being there for you; rather it serves as both a source of wisdom for you... AND for you to be a source of support and inspiration for them as well; it is a mutually beneficial relationship.

Friends and Family
The idea of 'birds of a feather flock together' doesn't just work in the negative. It also proves

true in the positive sense as well. Surrounding yourself with others who have a positive outlook is a great way to alter a pessimistic mindset and create a healthy environment; hang around them long enough and before long you'll find you have developed a positive way of thinking too.

There have been a number of studies done highlighting the importance of having encouraged and supportive friends to one's emotional, mental and physical well-being. Not only does it boost your immune system, but it has also been found that supportive relationships can assist in the achievement of one's personal goals; this, is due to the continual encouragement along your journey, which helps to consistently motivate you and boost your willpower.

Organized Meetups

It is critical to engage in positive, encouraging and intellectually stimulating company of like-minded individuals. In our current digital age, this is very simple to do… many times without even leaving the house. Nevertheless, whether done online or at a pre-arranged location, there are clubs, organizations, and support groups that meet according to their group's set policies. It could be once a quarter, monthly, weekly, or daily with the basic premise being to provide support for one another.

Get a Mentor

As my Great-grandmother Lizzie has shared with me in the past, people become grown and believe that since they are adults they no longer need any one or require any guidance.

As the kids say… 'they got this!"

This is unfortunate. Because, when you determine that you don't need anyone's help and that you possess all the knowledge and counsel you will ever need, you are leaving something extremely valuable on the table that could easily serve you well.

Mentors aren't individuals who just tell you what to do; instead, they are persons with direct experience and first-hand knowledge who can recognize your weakness and support your growth and development.

Albert Einstein himself said, *"The more I learn, the more I realize how much I don't know."*

There are many benefits and advantages to acquiring the assistance of a mentor, such as wise counsel, direction, improved skill and access to contacts and resources not available to you otherwise or that you weren't aware even existed!

STOP WASTING YOUR TIME! If you are making a decision in any area of your life, business or personal, make sure to enlist the assistance of a circle of faithful friends or trusted advisors with whom you can share the details and be open to consider their words of wisdom and advice. This is a principle I have perfected in my personal and business life, which I learned from my elders and it has never failed to secure me and keep me safe from various obstacles and pitfalls along my journey.

"Without counsel purposes are disappointed: but in the multitude of counsellors they are established." ~Proverbs 15:22

CONCLUSION

I've always had the blessing of being surrounded by those who made it a point to not waste their time. Even this many years past, I can easily recall waking up around 4 – 4:30 in the morning to the sounds of my Great-grandmother and mother humming hymns and spirituals as they prepared the household for the day to come; the floors creaking under family member's footsteps, and the dried wood popping in the iron stove that set in the middle of the floor to heat the house.

I was about four or five years old and by the time I had gotten dressed and grabbed my cocker-sack-bag to put the cotton in from the field, I could hear my grandfather crying, "sooie pig" while he slopped the hogs with the leftover food from our meals the day before and milked the cows.

It was my mother who patiently taught me how to separate the bulb from the boll. She even told me then, "you may not be able to do as much as everyone else, but you will learn to work." They didn't rush me, but they made sure to come back and check on me every so often to confirm that I was doing okay and that I had water to drink... saying, "Keep going. We don't want to see you sitting down until we sit down." We all worked. No matter how small you were, you were given something to do. Over time, I learned to plant sweet potatoes, then later, soap making, farming vegetables, and driving a tractor.

Our family made use of everything; and not just for our family, but for the community as well. The only thing we went to the store for was flour.

What this taught me, from a very young age, was to always be thinking about what to do with my life; to not be idle, but productive. The legacy I received from this experience was to have an entrepreneurial mindset and to not waste any of my time.

This is my foundation: Ahead of time thinking. This is the foundation for everything I am and everything I do. It is the same knowledge I impart to those I get the opportunity to coach and mentor and it is the basis for every lesson I share with those I come into contact.

From this, I developed a plan... and, this plan is something I review daily, making sure to put feet to my thoughts; knowing that the vision will produce income for me if I develop it!

Proper Preparation with Persistence

Leaves you an

Advantage

Never without options

Let me share this final thought with you... Remove the word *can't* from your vocabulary. Instead:

STOP WASTING YOUR TIME AND FIND A WAY!

I'm Mr. 1% Unlimited Thinker... and I'm out!

ABOUT THE AUTHOR

Dr. Michael Miller, also known as Mr. 1% Unlimited Thinker, is the Founder and President of Then What Corporation; the parent organization that provides relevant principles and concepts to live by. This includes *Make The World A Better Place®*, which specializes in Manifesting your Purpose, Stop Wasting Your Time, and other legacy training tools, such as: Then What Decision Processes, 1%'ers Unlimited Thinking, and Mind Nutrition skills. A native of Reynolds, Georgia, Dr. Miller enlisted into the United States Air Force and retired after 20 years of exemplary service. It was in the Air Force where he was able to further develop his instinctive leadership ability.

While there, he served as a security forces specialist and administrative support to senior leaders on diverse personnel, leadership, and management issues. Throughout his military career, he realized an innate ability to motivate colleagues to plan a path into their own dreams in life.

Following retirement, Tampa, Florida became his home of residence. Miller was employed at Price Waterhouse Coopers as an information systems analyst and from there, launched out on his own to fulfill his entrepreneurial vision. As a motivational speaker, Dr. Miller inspires audiences to go beyond self-imposed barriers and discover their unique gifts and talents. Utilizing a practical and engaging style for his seminars, Miller inspires positive behavioral changes in the attendees... leaving them empowered.

Recognizing the gifts that he possessed, Miller went on to become the CEO of ThenWhat4U INC., a company endorsed by the Orlando Magic, which develops unique teaching products aimed at affirming people's self-worth and creating a mindset of unlimited thinking.

To locate your purpose and sphere of influence, contact Dr. Miller at:

www.stopwastingyourtime.org
Customers Thought page!!!

What ideas were valuable to your personal life that you will live by?

Please take your time to answer on this page and email us at stopwastingyourtime57@gmail.com so we may know how this book impacted you and your family life for the good. Thank you in advance for sharing your thoughts to help us grow.